Dear Student,

You are about to start a great adventure! This year, you are going to learn how to read Hebrew. By learning to read Hebrew you are taking your first big step toward fully being a part of the Jewish community.

Hebrew is the Jewish people's oldest language. It is the language of the Bible and Jewish prayer. It is also our newest language. Today in Israel, Hebrew is the language people speak. Hebrew has always held our people together, and when you learn Hebrew you link yourself to all Jews who have gone before you. As you begin to read Hebrew, you will learn some new Hebrew words and some words that are almost the same in Hebrew as they are in English.

Reading Hebrew can be a lot of fun. But Hebrew reading is a lot different from English reading. Here are some hints to help make Hebrew reading easier:

• English is read from left to right. We read Hebrew from right to left.

• Hebrew does not have capital letters, but there are five final letters in Hebrew. These are letter forms that are used only at the end of a word.

• In Hebrew, the name of the letter often tells you its sound. Learning the letter's name can help you remember the sound it makes.

• By reading every letter and every vowel, it is easy to sound out new Hebrew words.

• In Hebrew, the vowels are often tiny dots and dashes written under, over, or after the letters. People who know Hebrew can read without these markings.

• In Hebrew reading, tiny markings can be very important. You need to look closely at every letter and every vowel.

• When you chant Torah or pray in Hebrew, you will be reading out loud. So, it's a good idea to practice reading Hebrew out loud.

And now . . . it's
Time to Read Hebrew!

Lesson 1
KEY WORD:
שַׁבָּת

New Letters:

Shin   שׁ

Bet   ב

Tav   ת

New Vowels:

Both of these vowels make an **"ah"** sound.
(The doctor says, "Open your mouth and say 'ah.'")

A Roman Emperor asked Rabbi Joshua,
"Why does your שַׁבָּת dish always smell so good?"

Rabbi Joshua answered, "We have a special spice
called שַׁבָּת to give our meal a wonderful flavor."

The Emperor said, "Give me some of it."

"I'm sorry, it works for one who keeps שַׁבָּת but
not for anyone else," answered Rabbi Joshua.

(Talmud — *Shabbat* 119a)

Lesson 1
READING PAGE

KEY WORD: שַׁבָּת

.1	שָׁ	בְ	תַ	תָ
.2	שָׁבְ	שָׁתָ	בָתְ	בַּשְׁ
.3	בַּבְ	שָׁשָׁ	שַׁתְ	בַּתְ
.4	בַּב	שָׁשׁ	שַׁת	בַּת
.5	שָׁת	בְשׁ	בַּת	שַׁב
.6	שָׁשַׁת	בַּבְשׁ	שַׁבָּת	בְשַׁב
.7	בָּשַׁת	שַׁבְשׁ	בַּבַּת	שָׁבְשׁב

Cool Hebrew Words

daughter = בַּת

Lesson 1

KEY WORD: שַׁבָּת

Practice writing the letter Shin.

Now write the letter with this vowel.

Practice writing the letter Bet.

Now write the letter with the second vowel.

Practice writing the letter Tav.

Now write the letter with one of the vowels you have learned.

Circle the Key Word on the challah cover.

לִכְבוֹד שַׁבָּת וְיוֹם טוֹב

Lesson 1
KEY WORD: שַׁבָּת

Circle the letters that make the same sound as the letter on the right.

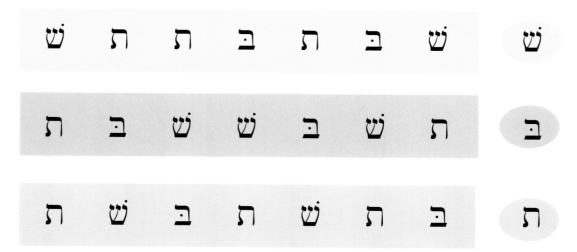

The Key Word is written twice in the box below. Find it both times and circle it.

שׁ ת ת שׁ ב ת שׁ ב ב שׁ ת ב שׁ

Write the Key Word on the challah covers.

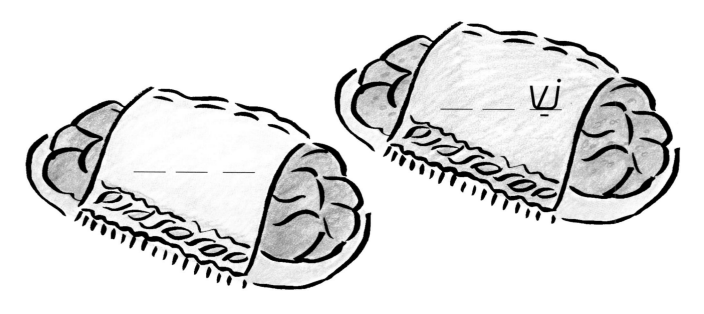

Lesson 1
KEY WORD: שַׁבָּת

With what sound does the picture start? Circle the correct letters.

Group Activity
Read the pairs in each
שַׁבָּת candle out loud
to your teacher.

בַּב
בַּב

בַּשׁ
בַּשׁ

שַׁשׁ
שַׁשׁ

בַּת
בַּת

שַׁת
שַׁת

שַׁב
שַׁב

Lesson 2
KEY WORD:
דָּג

New Letters:

Dalet ד

Gimel ג

This story about eating דָּג on שַׁבָּת comes from the Talmud.
A man named Joseph had a greedy neighbor. The neighbor
was told that Joseph would somehow get all his money.
So, the neighbor sold everything and bought one precious
jewel. He put the jewel into his turban to keep it safe.
One day, the wind blew the turban into the river. A דָּג
swallowed the jewel.

Weeks later, the דָּג was caught and brought to market.
When Joseph saw the דָּג, he bought it right away for
Shabbat. When he cut into the fish, he found the jewel
inside. Joseph sold the jewel for 13 rooms filled with gold
coins. And so it is said, if you honor Shabbat, שַׁבָּת will
repay you with honor.

(Talmud — *Shabbat* 119a)

Lesson 2
READING PAGE

KEY WORD: דָּג

דְ	תָ	בַ	גָ	שֶׁ	.1
גְָג	גְָד	גַָב	גְָת	גְָשֶׁ	.2
גַג	גַד	גַב	גַת	גַשׁ	.3
תָּד	דָד	דְָג	דָתָ	דַשׁ	.4
תַּד	דַד	דָג	דַת	דַשׁ	.5
שֶׁתָ	שָׁשׁ	בַָג	תַָג	שְָׁג	.6
שֶׁת	שָׁשׁ	בֵָג	תַָג	שָׁג	.7

Cool Hebrew Words

religion = דָּת

Lesson 2
READING PAGE

KEY WORD: דָּג

בַּגַת	בַּדַת	בֶּגֶד	בַּדְגָ	בַּדְשׁ	.1
גַת	דַת	גַד	דַג	דָשׁ	.2
דַגַת	גַדַת	בֶּגֶד	בַּדְג	גַדְשׁ	.3
שַׁגַת	שֶׁדַת	תַגְד	שַׁדְג	תַּדְשׁ	.4
תַג	בָּד	גַשׁ	נַג	בֶּג	.5
בַּתַג	שַׁבַּד	דַגְשׁ	בַּגַג	בַּבֶּג	.6
שָׁתַג	דָבַד	בָּגַשׁ	שַׁגַג	שֶׁבַּג	.7

9

Lesson 2
KEY WORD: דָג

Practice writing the letter Dalet.

Practice writing the letter Gimel.

Practice writing the Key Word.

On each line circle every Hebrew letter that matches the English sound on the right.

ד	ב	ג	שׁ	ת		**T**
שׁ	ד	ב	ת	ג		**SH**
ת	ד	ג	ד	ב		**D**
ב	שׁ	ת	ד	ג		**G**
ד	ב	שׁ	ג	ת		**B**

Lesson 2

KEY WORD: דָּג

Color in every:

D sound in **red**

G sound in **green**

B sound in **blue**

T sound in **yellow**

SH sound in **purple**

Go fishing! Draw a fish around every דָּג in the tank.

How many fish did you catch? _____

Lesson 2

KEY WORD: דָּג

The objects below are called the same thing in Hebrew and English.
Write the first sound of each word in Hebrew.

Finish setting the שַׁבָּת table.
Write the Key Words you know in their correct places.

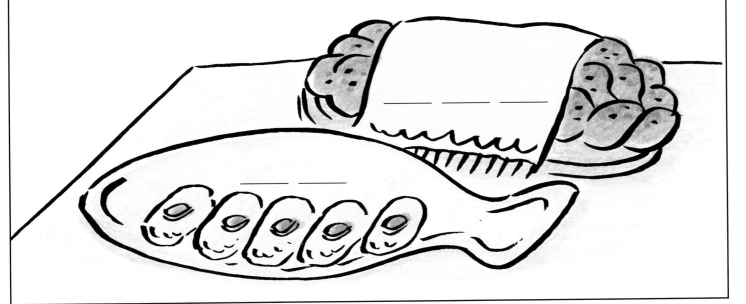

Lesson 3
KEY WORDS:
אִמָא   אַבָּא

New Letters:

(**silent** letter) Alef   א

Mem   מ

New Vowel:

It has the sound of "ee" as in see.

To honor אַבָּא and אִמָא is one of the
Ten Commandments. We are taught that
by obeying this commandment we are
worthy of a long life. This is the Torah's
way of telling us that to honor our
parents keeps the Jewish people alive.
When we follow this commandment, it is
as if we, too, are standing at Mount Sinai.

Lesson 3
READING PAGE

KEY WORDS:
אִמָא   אַבָּא

גְ	מְ	מֶ	אִ	אַ	.1
אָא	דָ	מָא	גָא	בָ	.2
אִשׁ	אָב	אַבְ	אָתְ	אַתָ	.3
דָא	בָא	שָׁא	תָא	גָא	.4
תִשׁ	מָת	אִת	מְשׁ	בַת	.5
תַשׁ	מָת	אַת	מָשׁ	בַת	.6
מְתָשׁ	בָּמְת	בָאְת	אִמְשׁ	אִבָת	.7

Cool Hebrew Words

helping candle = שַׁמָשׁ

Lesson 3
READING PAGE

KEY WORDS: אַבָּא   אִמָא

מַת	בַּת	גַד	מַד	גֵּשׁ	.1
מֵת	בֵּת	גֵד	מֵד	גֵּשׁ	.2
אָמַת	אַבָּת	אַגַד	אָמַד	אָגַשׁ	.3
תָמֵת	תַבֵּת	תָגֵד	תָמֵד	תָגֵשׁ	.4
אַשׁ	מֵשׁ	אַד	דַשׁ	מַג	.5
אָשׁ	מָשׁ	אָד	דָשׁ	מָג	.6
גָאֵשׁ	גָמֵשׁ	מָאַד	אָדֵשׁ	בַּמֵג	.7

15

Lesson 3

KEY WORDS: אַבָּא אִמָּא

Practice writing the letter Aleph.

אאאאא

Practice writing the letter Mem.

מ מ מ מ מ

Practice writing the letter Aleph with all of the vowels you have learned.

אִ אַ אָ

Match each picture to the correct sound.

Lesson 3
KEY WORDS: אַבָּא אִמָא

Vowel Hints

Sometimes the doctor tells you to open your mouth and say "Ah." Then the doctor puts a stick in your mouth. This stick is called a "tongue depressor," and it looks like this:

When you see a Hebrew vowel that is shaped like a stick, (or a stick with a handle), remember to say, "Ah."

The **"ee"** vowel is one dot under a letter. It looks like a little b**ea**d.

Draw a tongue depressor around all the words that have the "ah" sound in them.
Draw a bead around all the words that have the "ee" sound in them.

אִדְשׁ   בַּגֶד   מְשׁ תָא   גַג גָד

Aleph א is the first letter of the Hebrew alphabet.
Tav ת is the last letter of the Hebrew alphabet.
Color in the spaces that contain the first or last letter of the Hebrew alphabet.

גַג	דָגֵשׁ	דַשׁ	בֵּג	גָד
שַׁבָּת תָת	שַׁג שָׁג	אָג	דַב	דָא
דָג שָׁ תָ	בַּת	אַבָּא	אָ	אַשׁ בָּא ג
		גְבָשׁ	שָׁא	ד א
אָת	בַ דָת דְת	בַד	אַד	שַׁב גָא

Lesson 3

KEY WORDS: אַבָּא אִמָּא

Complete the pictures and the words. Color the pictures if you wish.

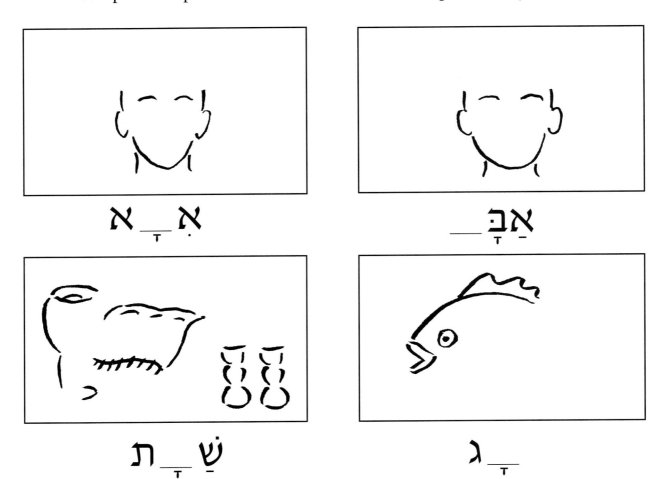

אִ _ָ א

אַ _ָבּ _

שַׁ _ָ ת

גַ _ָ

Write two Key Words under each picture.

א _ _ _

א _ _ _

Lesson 3
KEY WORDS: אַבָּא אִמָּא

Help אַבָּא and אִמָּא set up the nursery for their new baby.
Match each Hebrew letter with its sound.

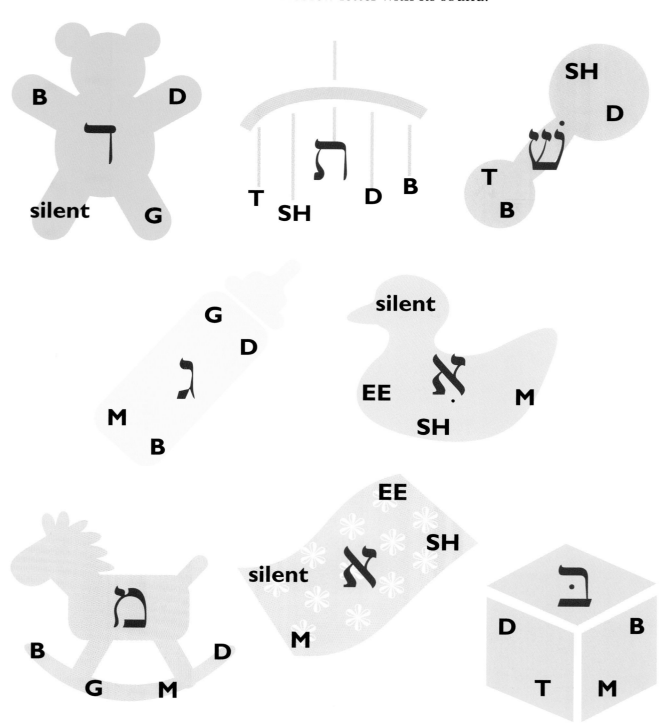

Lesson 4

KEY WORDS:

מַצָה הַגָדָה

New Letters:

Tsadi

 makes the sound of **"ts"** as in Be**ts**y.

Hey ה

READING CLUE

The sound of the letter ה is just like the English letter H.
When followed by a vowel, the ה is pronounced like the "H" in happy.
At the end of a word, the ה is silent.

The word הַגָדָה comes from the Hebrew word for telling a story. The הַגָדָה we read at the Passover Seder tells the story of how we left Egypt. מַצָה is one of the special foods in this story. The הַגָדָה tells us that the Hebrew slaves made cakes of מַצָה (unleavened bread) to eat on their journey.

Did you know that up until 150 years ago מַצָה was always round? That is because מַצָה was always made by hand. In 1857, a machine for making מַצָה was invented. But the machine could only make the מַצָה in a square shape. That's why most מַצָה we eat today is square.

Lesson 4
READING PAGE
KEY WORD:
הַגָּדָה

מַ	הֵ	דָ	גַ	הַ	1.
דָה	שָׁה	גָה	בָּ	מַה	2.
הָדָה	הַשָּׁה	הַגָּה	הַבָּה	הָמָה	3.
אִדָה	אִשָׁה	אִגָה	אִבָּה	אִמָה	4.
גְשָׁה	שָׂדָה	בָּתָה	מְדָה	אִתָּה	5.
בָּאָה	דָהָה	גָדָה	אַהָה	גָאָה	6.
הַשָּׁמָשׁ	הַבָּת	הָאִמָא	הַדָג	הַשַּׁבָּת	7.

Cool Hebrew Words

woman, wife = אִשָׁה

21

Lesson 4
READING PAGE

KEY WORDS:
מַצָּה הַגָּדָה

1.	צָדָה	צָמָה	צַתָה	אַצָה	צָמָא
2.	אָצָה	מִצָּה	בְּצָה	דְּצָה	גְּצָה
3.	מָד	מְד	צַד	מְג	צַת
4.	צֶמָד	צָמְד	בַּצָד	צָמְג	מִצָת
5.	מָגְד	דְצָת	מָגְש	בְּצָת	מַצָת
6.	הַגְּשָׁה	הִתְָשָׁה	הַצָתָה	הַגָּדָה	הַצְגָה
7.	הַגְּשֵׁת	הִתְָשֵׁת	הַצַתָת	הַגְדֵת	הַצָגֵת

22

Lesson 4

KEY WORD: מַצָּה

Practice writing the letter Hey.

ה ה ה ה

Practice writing the letter Tsadi.

צ צ צ

Practice writing the Key Word מַצָּה

מַצָּה

Circle the sound of צ in each of the following words:

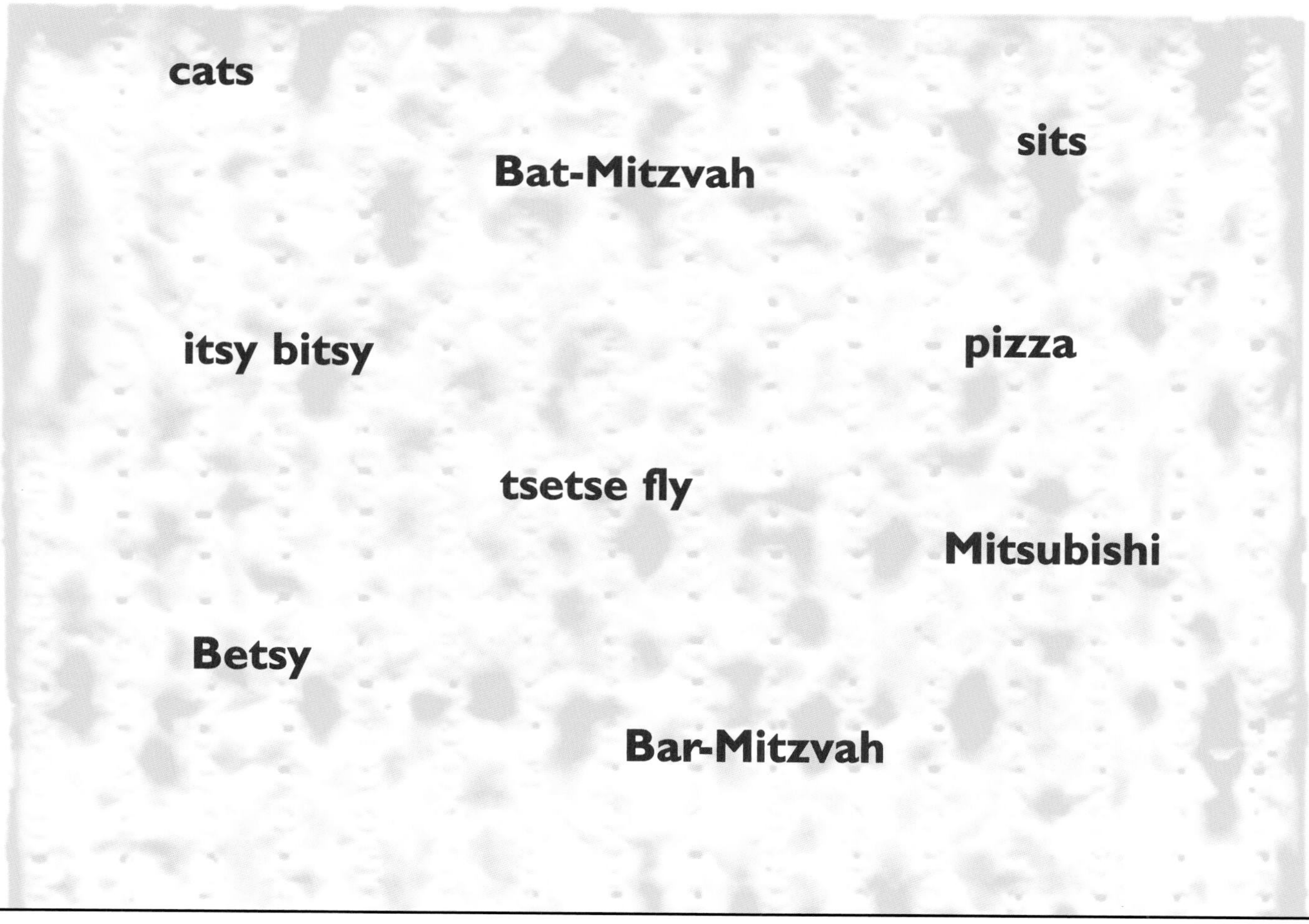

cats

Bat-Mitzvah

sits

itsy bitsy

pizza

tsetse fly

Mitsubishi

Betsy

Bar-Mitzvah

Lesson 4

KEY WORD: הַגָּדָה

At the Passover Seder, we spill a drop of wine to remember each of the ten plagues. Draw a line from each plague to a drop that matches. See the example.

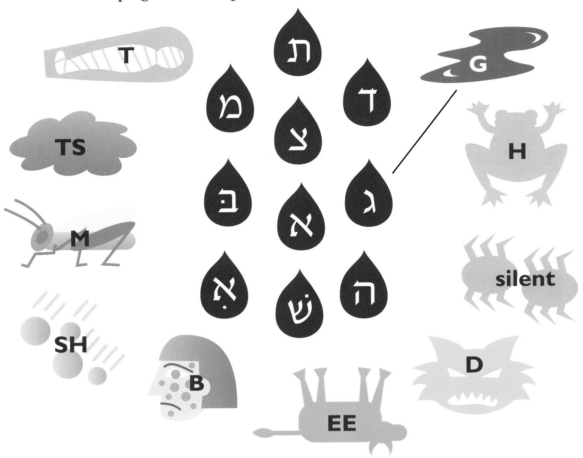

The הַגָּדָה tells the story of Passover.
Write the word הַגָּדָה under each picture that has to do with Passover.

Lesson 4

KEY WORDS: הַגָּדָה מַצָה

New Vocabulary

the = ___ הַ

In Hebrew הַ means "the."
You attach it to the front of a word.

the Shabbat = הַשַׁבָּת

the _____ = הַדָג

_____ matzah = הַמַצָה

In the Hebrew words above,
circle the Hebrew letter that means "the."

Note: Not every הַ at the start of a word means "the."
What word do you know that starts this way?

_____

Complete this puzzle in Hebrew. Do not use vowels.

Clues (across only)

1. The Sabbath

2. Fish

3. A book you read at the Passover seder

4. The bread you eat on Passover

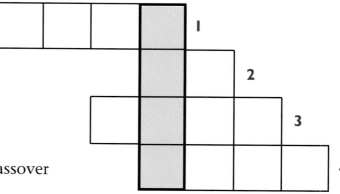

Draw a picture of the
word you found in the
shaded box reading down.

25

Lesson 5

KEY WORDS:

אֲנִי יָד

New Letters:

Nun נ

Yud יְ

READING CLUE

The letter י acts just like the English letter Y. Sometimes it's a vowel and sometimes it's a consonant. When the י is followed by a vowel, it makes the sound of "Y" as in "yes." Any other time, it is a vowel.

New Vowels:

■ = ■ = ■
ָ — ֵ:

י ■ = ■
ִ ִ

The word אֲנִי (I) appears many times in the Torah. God tells the Jewish people, "I am Adonai your God."

We use a special pointer called a יָד when reading the Torah. This יָד helps readers keep their place. Because it takes the place of a hand, it is often shaped like a יָד with a pointing finger.

KEY WORDS: אֲנִי יָד

יָג	יֵשׁ	יָה	יֵת	יָד	.1
דַיָג	תֵישׁ	מַיָה	בֵּית	מִיָד	.2
אִי	מִי	הִי	בִּי	דִי	.3
אִית	מִית	הִית	בֵּית	דִית	.4
תְנָה	מְנָה	דְנָה	בְּנָה	שָׁנָה	.5
תִינָה	מִינָה	דִינָה	בִּינָה	שִׁינָה	.6
אֲתִי	אֲצִי	אֲמִי	אֲדִי	אֲשִׁי	.7

Cool Hebrew Words

man = אִישׁ

ground, soil = אֲדָמָה

KEY WORDS: אֲנִי יָד

תָּמִי	גַּבִּי	מָתִי	גְּדִי	דָּנִי	.1
דָּיְג	מָיָה	צַיִד	צִיָּה	תַּיִשׁ	.2
גָּדִישׁ	תָּמִיד	אָדִישׁ	אָמִיד	גָּמִישׁ	.3
בָּנִיתָ	שָׁנִיתָ	הָגִיתָ	גָּנִיתָ	שָׁגִיתָ	.4
אֲמִידָה	אַגָּדָה	אֲדִישָׁה	אֲמָתִי	אֲדָמָה	.5
הַצָּגָה	נָצִיג	הִצִּיג	יָצִיג	אַצִּיג	.6
הַגָּדָה	נָגִיד	הִגִּיד	יָגִיד	אַגִּיד	.7

Cool Hebrew Words

a tallit fringe = צִיצִת

year = שָׁנָה

Lesson 5

KEY WORDS: אֲנִי יָד

Practice writing the letter Yud. Notice how small the Yud is.

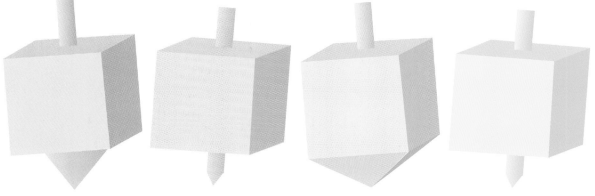

Practice writing the letter Nun.

Fill in the four letters that appear on dreidels used outside of Israel.

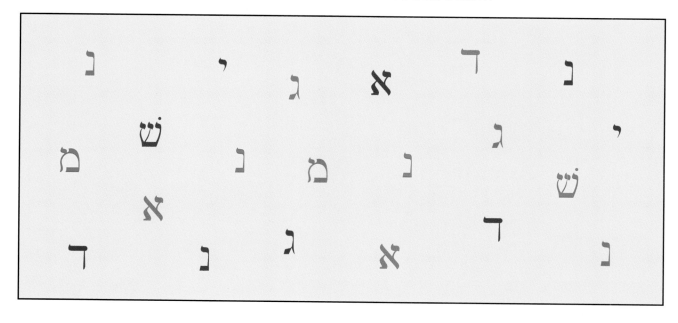

These letters stand for: "A Big Miracle Happened There."

Circle each Nun letter in the box below.

נ		י		ג		א		ד		נ
מ		שׁ		נ		מ		נ		ג		י
ד		א		נ		ג		א		ד		שׁ
												נ

Lesson 5
KEY WORDS: אֲנִי יָד

Write the Key Word יָד next to each correct picture.

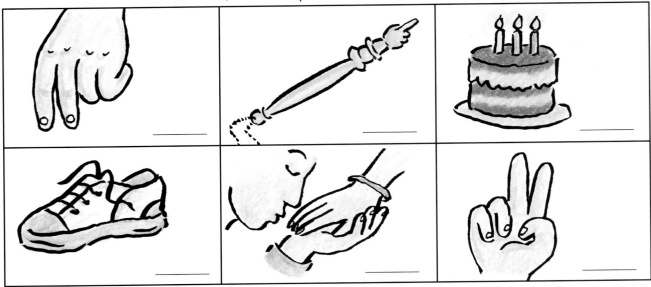

In each line below, cross out the word that you think does not belong.
Hint: Pay attention to the meaning of the words.
Example:

מַצָּה ~~אַבָּא~~ הַגָּדָה

1. בַּנָנָה מַצָּה יָד

2. אֲנִי דָג שַׁבָּת

3. אֲנִי אִמָּא הַגָּדָה

Lesson 5

KEY WORDS: אֲנִי יָד

Does the letter י make a consonant sound or a vowel sound
in the words below? Put a check in the correct column.
Two examples have been done for you.

י is a vowel	י is a consonant		
✔		אֲנִי	1
	✔	יָד	2
		אִישׁ	3
		דָנִי	4
		מִיָד	5
		מִי	6
		צִיצִית	7
		מִידָה	8
		בַּיִת	9
		דִינָה	10
		דָיָג	11
		יַבָּשָׁה	12

אֲנִי דָנִי

אֲנִי מַיָה

Danny

Maya

31

Lesson 5

KEY WORDS: יָד אֲנִי

Circle all the Hebrew letters on each line that sound the same as the sound on the right.

ג	ד	ד	י	ד	**D**
ת	ד	ה	ב	ת	**T**
ג	נ	ד	ג	י	**G**
ת	צ	צ	מ	ג	**TS**
י	נ	ג	מ	נ	**N**
נ	ב	ת	ב	ה	**B**
שׁ	ת	שׁ	נ	שׁ	**SH**
י	י	ה	י	ד	**Y**
מ	מ	י	מ	נ	**M**
נ	ה	ד	ת	ה	**H**
אֲ	א	צֲ	אֲ	אֲ	**אֲ**

32

Lesson 5
KEY WORDS: אֲנִי יָד

New Vocabulary

who (is)? = מִי?

Circle the picture that best answers each question.

מִי דָנִי?   מִי אִמָא?   מִי אַבָּא?

מִי אַבָּא?   מִי אִמָא?   מִי דָנִי?

Answer the questions above by filling in what each person would reply.
Use the words in the answer box below.

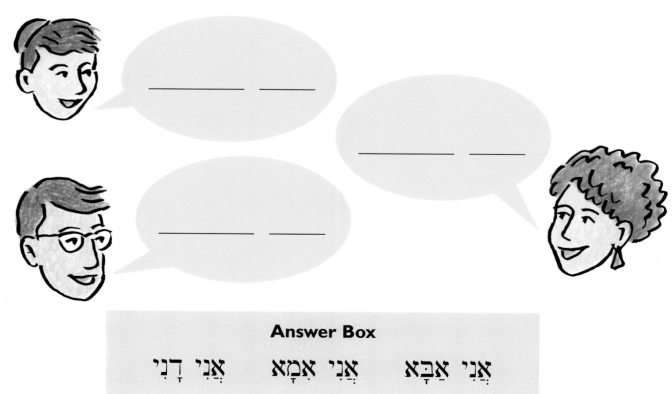

_____ _____

_____ _____

_____ _____

Answer Box

אֲנִי אַבָּא   אֲנִי אִמָא   אֲנִי דָנִי

33

Lesson 5

KEY WORDS: אֲנִי יָד

New Vocabulary

בַּיִת = (house)

בַּ = ___ in the

בַּבַּיִת = in the house

Read the Hebrew under each picture. Then complete each picture.

אֲנִי בַּבַּיִת   אַבָּא בַּבַּיִת   אִמָּא בַּבַּיִת   הַבַּיִת

Circle the correct answer to each question.

מִי בַּבַּיִת?

דָּנִי בַּבַּיִת
אַבָּא בַּבַּיִת
אִמָּא בַּבַּיִת

מִי בַּבַּיִת?

אַבָּא בַּבַּיִת
אִמָּא בַּבַּיִת
דָּנִי בַּבַּיִת

מִי בַּבַּיִת?

אִמָּא בַּבַּיִת
אַבָּא בַּבַּיִת
אֲנִי בַּבַּיִת

Lesson 5
KEY WORDS:
אֲנִי יָד

PREPARE for PRAYER

Once you have finished the *Time to Read Hebrew* workbooks, you will be ready to read the Siddur (prayer book). You can read quite a few words from the Hebrew prayer book now. On "Prepare for Prayer" pages, you will get extra practice with the kinds of words that are in the Siddur.

GO UP TO THE בִּימָה

Start in the lower right-hand corner and read all the words in each stair to a partner. If you make a mistake, start over again. Keep trying until you can climb all the way up to the בִּימָה without making a mistake.

7. בִּימָה

6. צִיצִת שִׁשָּׁה הָאֲדָמָה

5. תָּמִיד הָיִיתָ הָיִיתִי הָיָה

4. נָתַתָּ נָתַתִּי שִׁשִּׁי נַגִּיד יַגִּיד

3. אִמִּי בִּינָה אִתִּי אִישׁ הִיא

2. יָצָא אָנָה אֲנָא אָנָּא נָא

1. בַּיִת בָּא בָּהּ שַׁבָּת בַּת

35

Lesson 6

KEY WORDS:

קָדוֹשׁ   יַיִן

New Letters:

Koof   ק

Final Nun   --ן--

New Vowels:

וֹ has the sound of "oo" as in "boo."

New Combination:

וֹי has the sound of "ooey."

On שַׁבָּת and holidays, we lift up a cup of יַיִן and say the קָדוֹשׁ blessing to make the day special. Long ago, קָדוֹשׁ was said only at home before the meal. Later, we began to say the blessing over יַיִן during the Friday evening service. Why? Because travelers often stayed in the synagogue for שַׁבָּת and ate their meals there. Joining them for קָדוֹשׁ was one way the community welcomed its visitors.

Because יַיִן cost a lot of money, one cup was shared by all. This custom is still followed in many homes today.

Lesson 6
READING PAGE
KEY WORD:
קָדוֹשׁ

הוּא	צוּ	בּוּ	אוּ	קוּ	.1
מוּ	גוּ	יוּ	דוּ	נוּ	.2
הָמוּ	דָּגוּ	הָיוּ	קָדוּ	אָנוּ	.3
קוּצִי	מוּקִי	נוּמִי	שׁוּקִי	קוּמִי	.4
תּוּשׁ	דּוּג	גוּשׁ	יוּד	צוּד	.5
נָתוּשׁ	אָדוּג	דָּגוּשׁ	צִיוּד	נָצוּד	.6
יַגִּידוּ	יָצִיצוּ	קָנִינוּ	יָצוּמוּ	יָקוּמוּ	.7

Cool Hebrew Words

marketplace = שׁוּק

Lesson 6
READING PAGE

KEY WORDS: קָדוֹשׁ   יַיִן

יָן	קֵן	גַן	מָן	נָן	.1
יַיִן	קֵין	גִין	מִין	נִין	.2
צִיוֹן	תִּקוֹן	נִגוֹן	אָמוֹן	שָׁנוֹן	.3
מִיוֹן	שִׁקוֹן	תָּגוֹן	תָּמוֹן	גָנוֹן	.4
אֲשִׁינוֹת	אֲגִידָה	אֲנִינוֹת	אֲגוּדָה	אֱמָתִי	.5
גְנוּי	מְצוּי	שָׁנוּי	נְקוּי	מְנוּי	.6
נָדוֹן	דִּיוֹן	דַיָן	דָן	דִין	.7

Cool Hebrew Words

garden = גַן

Lesson 6

KEY WORDS: קָדוֹשׁ יַיִן

Notice that the final Nun drops below the line. ן

Remember! A Nun that is not final looks like this: נ

Practice writing the name of the letter.

נוּן

Practice writing the letter Koof.

ק ק ק

Circle every cup that contains the sound of the letter **K**.

Lesson 6

KEY WORDS: קִדּוּשׁ יַיִן

Write the correct Nun in the following words.

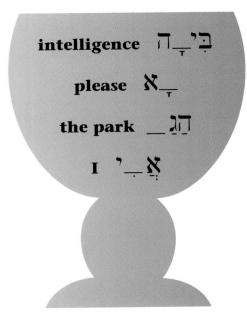

intelligence בִּי__ָה

please __ָא

the park __הַגַ

I אֲ__ִי

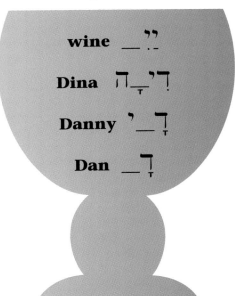

wine __יַ

Dina דִי__ָה

Danny דָ__ִי

Dan דָ__

This Nun appears only at the end of a word: _____

This Nun appears at the start or middle of a word: _____

Read the combinations below.

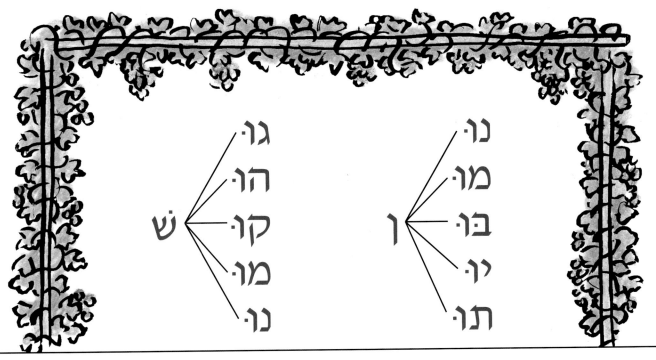

גוּ
הוּ
שׁ · קוּ
מוּ
נוּ

נוּ
מוּ
ן · בוּ
יוּ
תוּ

Lesson 6

KEY WORDS: קָדוֹשׁ יַיִן

Color purple the spaces with words that have the sound of **N**.
Color silver the spaces with words that have the sound of **K**.

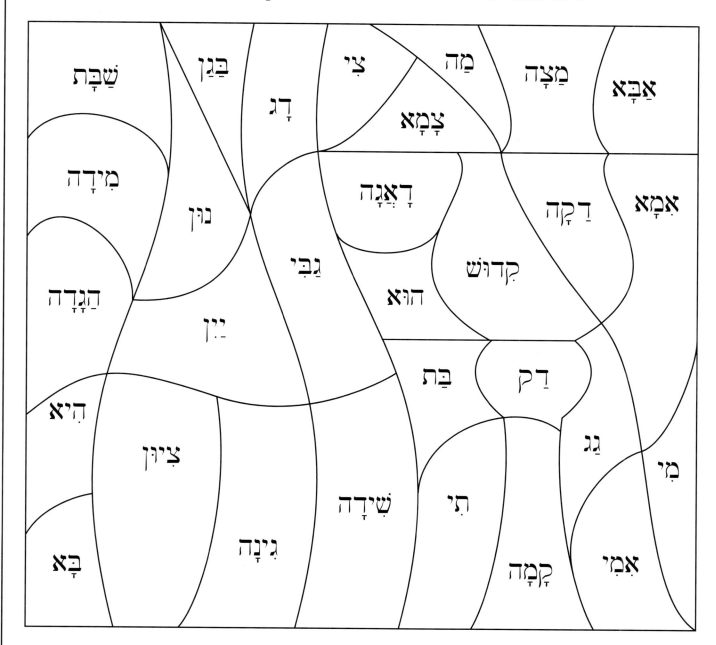

You put ___ __ יַ____ in the silver object every Friday evening

and recite the ___ ___ ___ קְ

Lesson 6
KEY WORDS: יַיִן קָדוֹשׁ

New Vocabulary
what (is)? = מָה?

מִי? or מַה?

Fill in the blanks with the best question word.
Look back to page 33 if you need help.

מַה _____

42

Lesson 6
KEY WORDS:
קָדוֹשׁ יַיִן

PREPARE for PRAYER

FOUR IN A ROW

Play this game with partners or class teams. One person or team is "X,"
the other is "O." Take turns reading the Hebrew in any box below.
If you read correctly, mark the box with your X or O. The first to get
four boxes in a straight line (up, down, or sideways) is the winner.

מַתָּן	נָתַן	דְּמָן	הָמָן	יַיִן
הַהוּא	הוּא	הַשָּׁנָה	בַּשָּׁנָה	שָׁנָה
בָּאוּ	אִתָּנוּ	תָּמוּ	בָּנוּ	אָנוּ
קַדִּישָׁא	קַדִּישׁ	קוּמָה	קוּמִי	קָמוּ
יַגִּידוּ	יַגִּיד	הַדִּין	בַּדִּין	דִּין
בַּצִּיצִית	הַצַּדִּיק	מַאֲמִין	וּמִין	מִן
אַיִן	הָיוּ	דַּיָּן	מִיַּיִן	הַיַּיִן

43

Lesson 7

KEY WORD:
פּוּרִים

  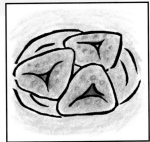 

New Letters:

Pey   פּ פ

Resh   ר

Final **M**em   ם

People often flip a coin or draw names out of a hat to make choices. Picking names is one way of "drawing lots."

The name of one of our happiest holidays comes from drawing lots or numbers. The Hebrew word פּוּרִים means "lots." How did this holiday get its name? The Megillah tells us that Haman drew פּוּרִים to pick a date to kill all the Jews of Persia. That date was the 14th of Adar. But we all know that it was Haman who had lots of trouble on that day!

Lesson 7
READING PAGE
KEY WORD:
פּוּרִים

פֶּה	רוּ	פָּא	רִי	פָ	.1
קַר	פַּת	רַק	פַּג	רְשׁ	.2
פָּנָה	קוּפָּה	מַפָּה	פּוּנָה	פֶּשָׂה	.3
רִנָה	פִּינָה	צָפָה	פִּיצָה	פִּיתָה	.4
בָּנוּי	אָפוּק	צָפוּי	פּהוּק	פָּצוּי	.5
אֲרָמִית	נוּרִית	רוּתִי	צוּרִי	אוּרִי	.6
יַאֲמִינוּ	יַאֲמִין	נַאֲמִין	מַאֲמִינָה	מַאֲמִין	.7

Cool Hebrew Words

Adar, the Hebrew month in which Purim comes = אֲדָר

45

Lesson 7
READING PAGE
KEY WORD:
פּוּרִים

.1	אִם	קָם	בּוּם	גַּם	צִים
.2	נָדַם	פָּדַן	אֲגַם	דָּגָן	קָדַם
.3	רָשׁוּם	הָמוּם	רָקוּם	פָּגוּם	פָּרוּם
.4	רַבִּים	קָצִין	אִירָן	קָמִים	רַבִּין
.5	בְּיוֹם	מָקוֹם	קִיוּם	קָדוּם	אִיוּם
.6	גַּפַּיִם	יָדַיִם	שְׁנַיִם	קַבַּיִם	אַפַּיִם
.7	יָרַד	יָרוּד	יָרִיד	רָדָה	דַּיָּר

Cool Hebrew Words

face = פָּנִים

Adam, the first human = אָדָם

Lesson 7
KEY WORD: פּוּרִים

Practice writing the letter Pey.

פ פ פ

Practice writing the letter Resh.

ר ר ר

Practice writing both forms of the Mem.

מ ם

Fill in the correct Mem:

Get up!	קוּ __
Water	__ יִ __
Boy's name	רְ __ יָ
Purim	פּוּרִי __
Said	אָ __ ר
Haman	הָ __ ן

Lesson 7
KEY WORD: פּוּרִים

New Vocabulary

רַבִּי =

Circle all the letters that have the sound of the letter **P**.

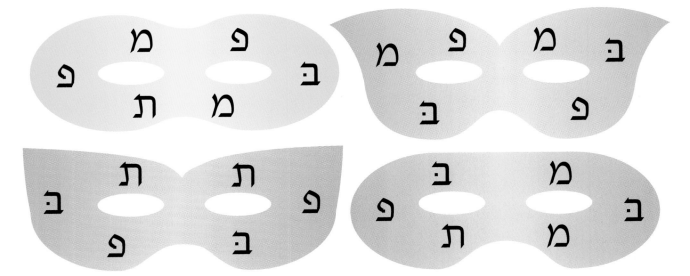

"Eat" the hamentaschen that **do not** contain the sound
of the letter **R** by crossing them out. Copy over the rest of
the words on the line below to answer the question.

What is Rami's costume?

_____   _____

Lesson 7
KEY WORD: פוּרִים

In each gragger below, circle every Hebrew letter
that matches the English sound-alike.

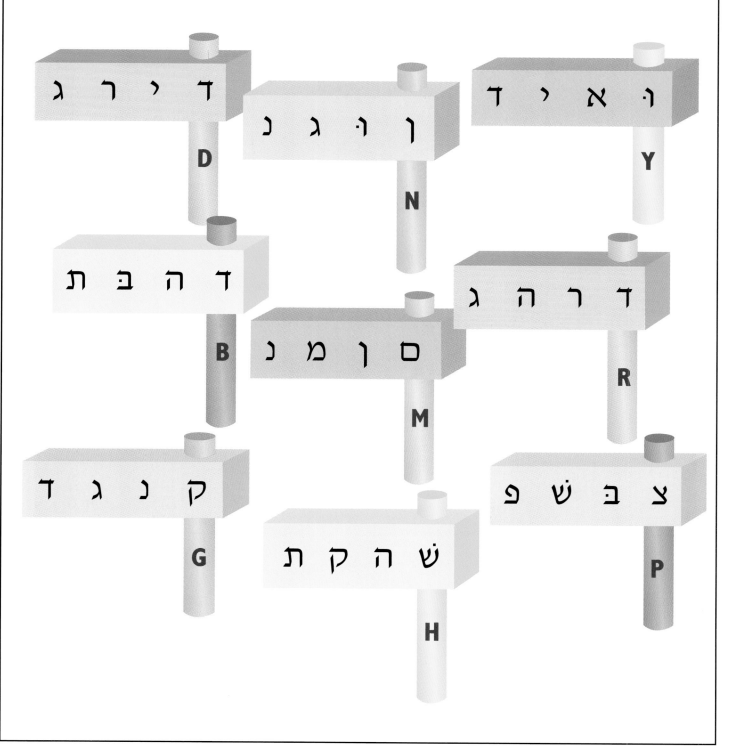

Lesson 7

KEY WORD: פּוּרִים

The names for the objects below are the same in Hebrew and English.
With which Hebrew letter does each object begin?

Lesson 7
KEY WORD: פּוּרִים

New Vocabulary

מַיִם

גִיר

Circle the word or sentence that matches each picture.

דָג בַּמַיִם
פּוּרִים בַּבַּיִת
יַיִן בְּיָד

אִמָא
מַיִם
יַיִן

דָג
גִיר
יָד

Make the question and answer describe the picture.
Fill in each blank with the correct word from the word box.

1. מַה בְּיָד? _____ בְּיָד.

2. מִי בַּבַּיִת? אַבָּא _____.

3. מַה בַּמַיִם? _____ בַּמַיִם.

4. _____ בְּיָד? גִיר בְּיָד.

5. _____ בַּבַּיִת? רוּת בַּבַּיִת.

Word Box

בַּבַּיִת

מַה

מִי

דָג

פִּיצָה

51

Lesson 7

KEY WORD: פּוּרִים

רוּת: אֲנִי דָג.

דָן: אֲנִי הָמָן.

רִמִי: אֲנִי רַבִּי. בּוּ הָמָן!

Write what each child says in the balloon.
Write the children's Hebrew names below their pictures.

אֲנִי _____

_____ _____

_____ _____

_____ _____ _____

The children are in costume because it is _____ .

Lesson 7
KEY WORD: פּוּרִים

רָם	פֻּר	יָם	הָר	דָם	.1
רָמִים	פֻּרִים	יָמִים	הָרִים	דָמִים	.2
בָּנִים	פָּנִים	בְּיָמִים	נָשִׁים	קָמִים	.3
בָּרָא	פָּנָה	רָצָה	רָאָה	קָרָא	.4
בָּרָאתִי	פָּנִיתִי	רָצִיתִי	רָאִיתִי	קָרָאתִי	.5
בָּרָאתָ	פָּנִיתָ	רָצִיתָ	רָאִיתָ	קָרָאתָ	.6
בָּרָאנוּ	פָּנִינוּ	רָצִינוּ	רָאִינוּ	קָרָאנוּ	.7

Cool Hebrew Words

call out, read = קָרָא

Look closely at the first word in lines 4 to 7. Each of these
words is like the word קָרָא (call out or read).

How are the two meanings of קָרָא related? Long ago,
reading was always something that was done out loud.

Lesson 8

KEY WORD:
חַלָה

New Letters:

Chet ח
(ch as in Chanukah)

Lamed ל

תּ = ת

On שַׁבָּת and holidays, the חַלָה is blessed after קִדוּשׁ is said. It is a custom to keep the חַלָה covered until we recite the blessing over the wine. Why? So that the חַלָה will not feel bad that we are saying the blessing for the יַיִן first. If we care for the feelings of an object, how much more should we care about the feelings of family, friends, and guests!

Lesson 8
READING PAGE
KEY WORD: חַלָּה

חַם	פַּח	חַג	אָח	חָשׁ	.1
חוּם	פָּחַד	חוּג	אַחַר	חוּשׁ	.2
רָחוּם	פָּרַח	יָחוּג	אַחִים	נָחוּשׁ	.3
לָצוּם	תָּלוּל	תָּלוּשׁ	לָקוּם	תָּקוּם	.4
חָלוּד	מָחוּל	לַחוּשׁ	לָחוּת	חָלוּל	.5
חֲלוּדָה	חֲלוּקָה	חֲקִירָה	חֲתִימָה	חֲצִיצָה	.6
חֲמִיצָה	חֲגִיגָה	חֲמִימוּת	חֲתִירָה	תַּפּוּחִים	.7

Cool Hebrew Words

life = חַיִּים

wedding canopy = חוּפָּה

55

Lesson 8

KEY WORD: חַלָה

Practice writing the letter Chet.

Practice writing the letter Lamed.

Practice writing the Key Word from this lesson.

The words for the objects below are the same in Hebrew and English.
Write the first Hebrew letter of each word on the correct line.

Lesson 8

KEY WORD: חַלָה

In each oval, cross out the words or pictures that **do not** belong.

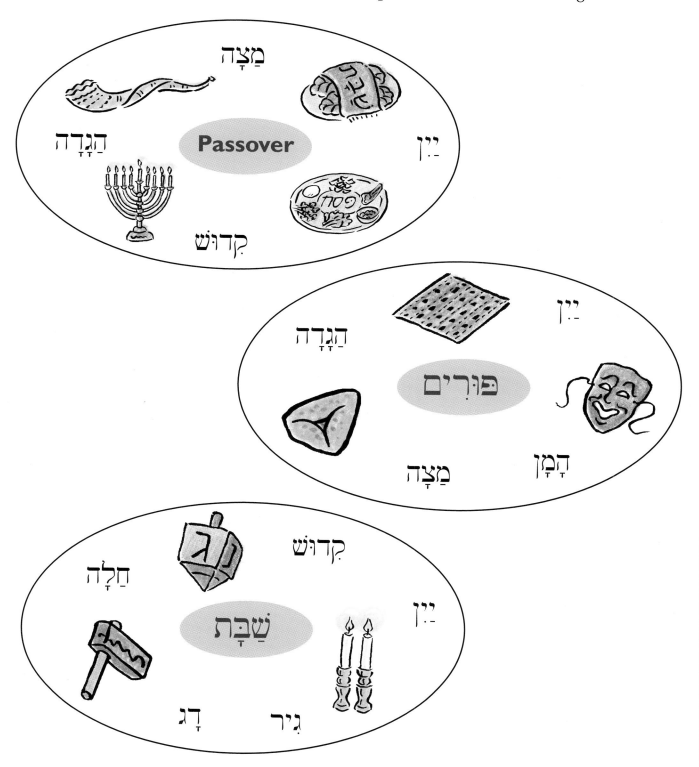

Lesson 8
KEY WORD: חַלָּה

Fill in the blanks with

אֲנִי אַתָּה מִי

or the person's name.

New Vocabulary

you (m.) = אַתָּה

Lesson 8
KEY WORD: חַלָה

New Vocabulary

under = תַחַת

Write the correct letter next to the matching question and answer.

1. מַה תַחַת הַיָד?

דָג תַחַת הַיָד.

2. מַה תַחַת הַהַגָדָה?

מַצָה תַחַת הַהַגָדָה.

3. מַה תַחַת הַגִיר?

יָד תַחַת הַגִיר.

4. מִי בַמַיִם?

אַבָּא בַמַיִם.

5. מַה תַחַת הַחַלָה?

יָד תַחַת הַחַלָה.

59

Lesson 8
"A Wedding" חֲתוּנָה

New Vocabulary

חָתוּל =

חֲתוּלָה

חָתוּל

אֶרִיק חָתוּל. חַנָּה חֲתוּלָה.

אֶרִיק תַּחַת חוּפָּה.

הַחֲתוּנָה: אֶרִיק, רַבִּי, חַנָּה.

חַנָּה תַּחַת חוּפָּה.

Lesson 8
KEY WORD: חַלָּה

PREPARE for PRAYER

לְבָם	לִבִּי	לָנוּ	לָה	לִי	.1
מָחָר	בָּחַר	צָהַר	אַחַר	שָׁחַר	.2
הִצִּיל	הַצָּלָה	מַצִּילָה	וּמַצִּיל	מַצִּיל	.3
יְחוּד	יָחִיד	יַחַד	אֵחוּד	אַחַת	.4
גְּלוּלִים	גְּלוּיִים	בְּגָלוּי	גָּלוּי	גָּלָה	.5
חִמּוּם	חָמוּם	חוּם	חַמָּה	חַם	.6
רַחֲמִים	הָרַחוּם	רַחוּם	הָרַחֲמָן	רַחֲמָן	.7

Cool Hebrew Words

Mercy, Compassion = רַחֲמִים

The Merciful One = הָרַחֲמָן

In the Siddur, God is often called הָרַחֲמָן because God
has lots of רַחֲמִים (mercy). This means that if you do
something wrong, God will give you a second chance.

Lesson 9
KEY WORDS:
מִצְוָה   הַבְדָּלָה

   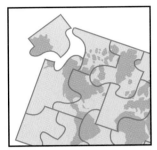

New Letters:

Vav   ו

Vet   ב

New Vowels:

֗ ֗ ֗   silent, ends the syllable

On Saturday night, we say good-bye to the holy day of שַׁבָּת by saying four blessings. This short service is called הַבְדָּלָה (separation). During the service, we use all five of our senses. We hear the blessings, smell sweet spices, and taste wine. We see the flame of a braided candle and feel its heat on our fingers.

It is a מִצְוָה (commandment) to make שַׁבָּת special. It is also a מִצְוָה to join in a הַבְדָּלָה service. Every מִצְוָה brings us closer to God. Every מִצְוָה makes us a partner with God in fixing the world.

Lesson 9
READING PAGE
KEY WORDS: מִצְוָה הַבְדָּלָה

The first six lines each contain one word written
three ways. Reading them will help you know
just how the ⬛ (the new silent vowel) works.

יַלְדָה	יַלְדָה	יַל דָה	.1
פָּתְחָה	פָּתְחָה	פָּת חָה	.2
פִּתְחָה	פִּתְחָה	פִּת חָה	.3
מִקְדָּשׁ	מִקְדָּשׁ	מִק דָשׁ	.4
נַקְדִּישׁ	נַקְדִּישׁ	נַק דִישׁ	.5
נָתְנוּ	נָתְנוּ	נָת נוּ	.6
לָמְדְנוּ	לָמְדוּ	לָמְדָה	לָמְדָה	.7
שָׁמַרְנוּ	שָׁמְרוּ	שָׁמְרָה	שָׁמְרָה	.8
גָּמַרְנוּ	גָּמְרוּ	גָּמְרָה	גָּמְרָה	.9

Cool Hebrew Words

Egypt = מִצְרַיִם

Lesson 9
READING PAGE

KEY WORDS:
מִצְוָה הַבְדָלָה

ב ָו = ָיו (at the end of a word)

שׁוּב	קָו	צָב	רַב	אַב	.1
שׁוּבִי	קָב	צַו	וָלָד	וָו	.2
צַוָּאר	צָבוּר	צָבָא	אֲוִיר	אֲבָל	.3
וִדּוּי	וָתִיק	וְרִיד	וְדָאוּת	וָדִי	.4
וַיִּקְרָא	נִבְרָא	קַוְּתָה	תִּקְוָה	שַׁלְוָה	.5
אֲהַבְתָּנוּ	אֲהַבְתִּי	אָהַבְתָּ	אַהֲבַת	מִצְוַת	מַבְדִּיל	.6
צַדִּיקָיו	תַּחְתָּיו	רַחֲמָיו	רַגְלָיו	בָּנָיו	.7

Cool Hebrew Words

we = אֲנַחְנוּ

"The Hope" (Israel's national anthem) = הַתִּקְוָה

Lesson 9

KEY WORDS: מִצְוָה הַבְדָּלָה

Practice writing the two letters that have the **V** sound.

ב ו

Circle every letter that makes the **V** sound.

בָּשָׁן

פֶּרְוָה תָּוִית

קָנוּ

בָּרִיא הַבְנָה

לְוִינוּ

שׁוּוק אָהוּב

בַּבַּיִת

רֵיק נָאוָה לִוְיָתָן

בָּנִים

דָּוִד חַוְיָה

חֲבִילָה

Lesson 9

KEY WORDS: מִצְוָה הַבְדָלָה

Write the Key Word הַבְדָלָה under the correct pictures.

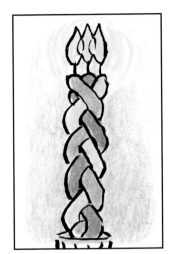

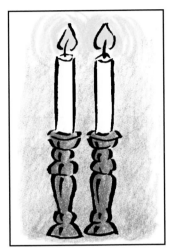

_____ 4 _____ 3 _____ 2 _____ 1

Write the Key Word מִצְוָה under the correct pictures.

_____ 4 _____ 3 _____ 2 _____ 1

Lesson 9

KEY WORDS: מִצְוָה, הַבְדָּלָה

Color the spaces with a **V** sound **violet** (or blue).
Color the spaces with an **R** sound **red**.
Color the spaces with a Y sound **yellow**.
Color the spaces with an **N** sound **green**.

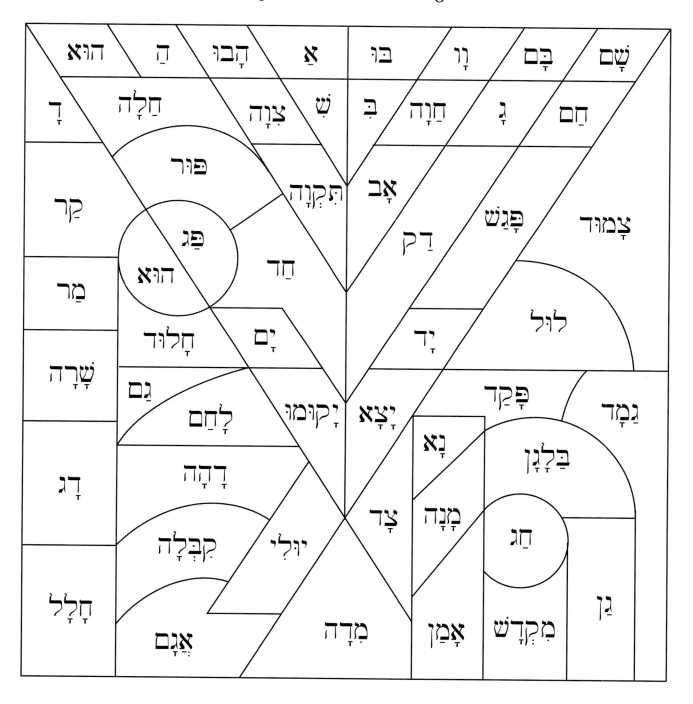

Lesson 9
KEY WORDS: מִצְוָה הַבְדָּלָה

Braid the הַבְדָּלָה candle. Connect the syllables to make Hebrew words that are also used in English. Use the clues on the right.

רִיל	הוּנ	Hungarian (a language)
דְלָה	פִּיק	lunch outdoors
נִיק	הַבְ	separation
וְה	שַׁמְ	for your hair
פּוּ	מִצְ	a commandment
חָק	אַבְ	the first Jew
רְהָם	יִצְ	his mother laughed
לוּ	מִנְ	ten Jews praying
יָן	אַגְ	an "ice" house
גְרִית	אַפְ	a spring month

Lesson 9

KEY WORDS: מִצְוָה הַבְדָּלָה

New Vocabulary

you (f.) = אַתְּ

Fill in the blanks with אַתְּ or אַתָּה or the person's name.

Lesson 9

KEY WORDS: מִצְוָה הַבְדָלָה

New Vocabulary

family = מִשְׁפָּחָה

Bar Mitzvah = בַּר-מִצְוָה

Bat Mitzvah = בַּת-מִצְוָה

Write the letter in each picture next to
its matching sentence below. (Hint:
There are more sentences than pictures.)

____ 1. דָג בַּמִשְׁפָּחָה.	____ 6. מִשְׁפָּחָה בַּמַיִם.
____ 2. מִי בַּבַּיִת?	____ 7. דָוִד בַּר-מִצְוָה.
____ 3. אֲבִיבָה בַּת-מִצְוָה.	____ 8. הַגִיר תַּחַת הַבַּיִת.
____ 4. מִשְׁפָּחָה בַּבַּיִת.	____ 9. חַלָה בַּבַּיִת.
____ 5. אַבָּא בַּבַּיִת.	____ 10. חַלָה בַּיָד.

Lesson 9
KEY WORDS:
מִצְוָה הַבְדָלָה

PREPARE for PRAYER

Hebrew words often come in families. Every member of a Hebrew word family has the same root. Most Hebrew roots have three letters. Members of a Hebrew word family all share a related meaning.

Read the words in each "word family tree."

אָהַב	קִוָה	מַבְדִיל
אַהֲבָה	הִקְוָה	הַמַּבְדִיל
אָהַבְתִּי	מִקְוֶה	הַבְדָלָה
אָהַבְתָּ	תִּקְוָה	הִבְדִיל
אֲהַבְתָּנוּ	הִתְקְוָה	הִבְדַלְתָּ

Separating   **Hoping**   **Loving**

___ ___ ___   ___ ___ ___   ___ ___ ___

Fill in the roots of each tree with its matching three-letter root.

ק.ו.ה   א.ה.ב   ב.ד.ל

Lesson 10

KEY WORDS:
עִבְרִית כִּתָּה

אוֹמֵר: יָפֶה תִּ
עָוֹן. וְכָל תּוֹרָה
עוֹסְקִים עִם הַ
מְסַיְּעֲתָם, וְצִדְקַ
כְּאִלּוּ עֲשִׂיתֶם.

New Letters:

Kaph   כ

(**silent** letter) Ayin   עַ

All Jews share the special gift of עִבְרִית (the Hebrew language). It is the language of Torah and of prayer. עִבְרִית is also the language spoken in Israel today. By learning עִבְרִית you connect yourself to all Jews everywhere.

In Israel, you can hear more than 100 different languages spoken by Jews. But they need to speak עִבְרִית in order to work and shop and eat. The early leaders of Israel formed an Ulpan, a kind of כִּתָּה for teaching עִבְרִית to new citizens. The lessons are taught using עִבְרִית only. Even children go to their own כִּתָּה in the Ulpan until they know enough עִבְרִית to begin regular classes.

Lesson 10
READING PAGE
KEY WORD:
עִבְרִית

אָם	עָם	עַם	רַע	עַד	.1
עָלוּב	לָווּ	עוּגָה	אֲבָל	וַעַד	.2
מַעְגָל	עָוִית	קָבוּעַ	אָבִיב	חָשׁוּב	.3
צַבְרִית	חֲבִילָה	צִבּוּר	חֲצוּבָה	צַבָּר	.4
בַּעֲלוּת	עֲבוּר	עוּגָב	עוּבָּר	עֲגָלָה	.5
עִנְיָן	מִבְצָע	נִלְהָב	מִבְצָר	מִצְעָד	.6
צִוּוּי	עוֹלָה	צִמְצוּם	לִבְלוּב	עַבְדוּת	.7

Cool Hebrew Words

week = שָׁבוּעַ

Lesson 10
READING PAGE

KEY WORDS:
עִבְרִית   כִּתָּה

.1	כּוּר	כָּאן	כּוּשׁ	קָרַע	כַּמָה
.2	כָּבוּל	כָּאַב	כַּדוּר	כָּבַשׁ	כְּעוּר
.3	עֲדַיִן	עַכָּבִישׁ	עֲרִיקָה	נַעֲמָן	עֲתִיקָה
.4	מִנְיָן	בִּנְיָן	חַקְיָן	בַּרְקָן	עֲבַרְיָן
.5	כְּפוֹר	כָּתוּב	כַּכָּתוּב	מִשְׁכָּן	בִּרְכַּת
.6	חִבַּרְתִּי	דְוַחְתִּי	עִיַּנְתִּי	כִּוַּנְתִּי	צִיַּרְתִּי
.7	הַרְצָאָה	מִבְרָקָה	הַשְׁוָאָה	מִבְרָאָה	מִצְבָּעָה

Cool Hebrew Words

kippah = כִּפָּה

Lesson 10

KEY WORDS: עִבְרִית כִּתָּה

Practice writing the two letters that have the **K** sound.

כֵּ קְ

Practice writing the letter Ayin.

עַ ע ע

Practice writing the two silent letters.

ע א

Circle the silent letters in the bulletin board.

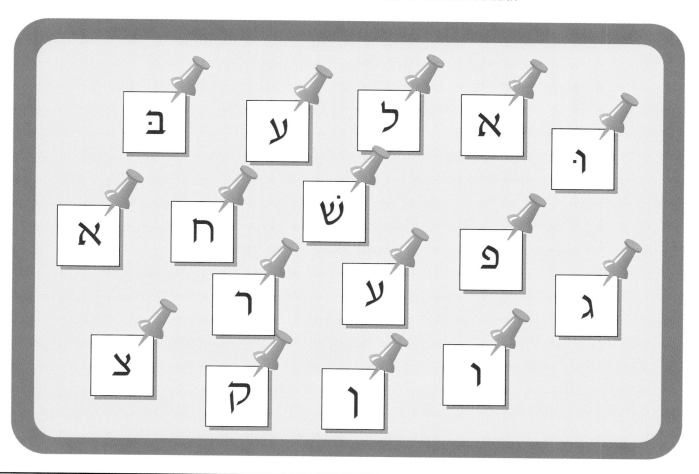

Lesson 10

KEY WORDS: עִבְרִית כִּתָּה

In the blank spaces write the Hebrew letters that sound the same.

____ = א   ____ = ק   ____ = ו

Match the tables and chairs for the כִּתָּה in the Ulpan.
Draw lines between the words that sound alike.

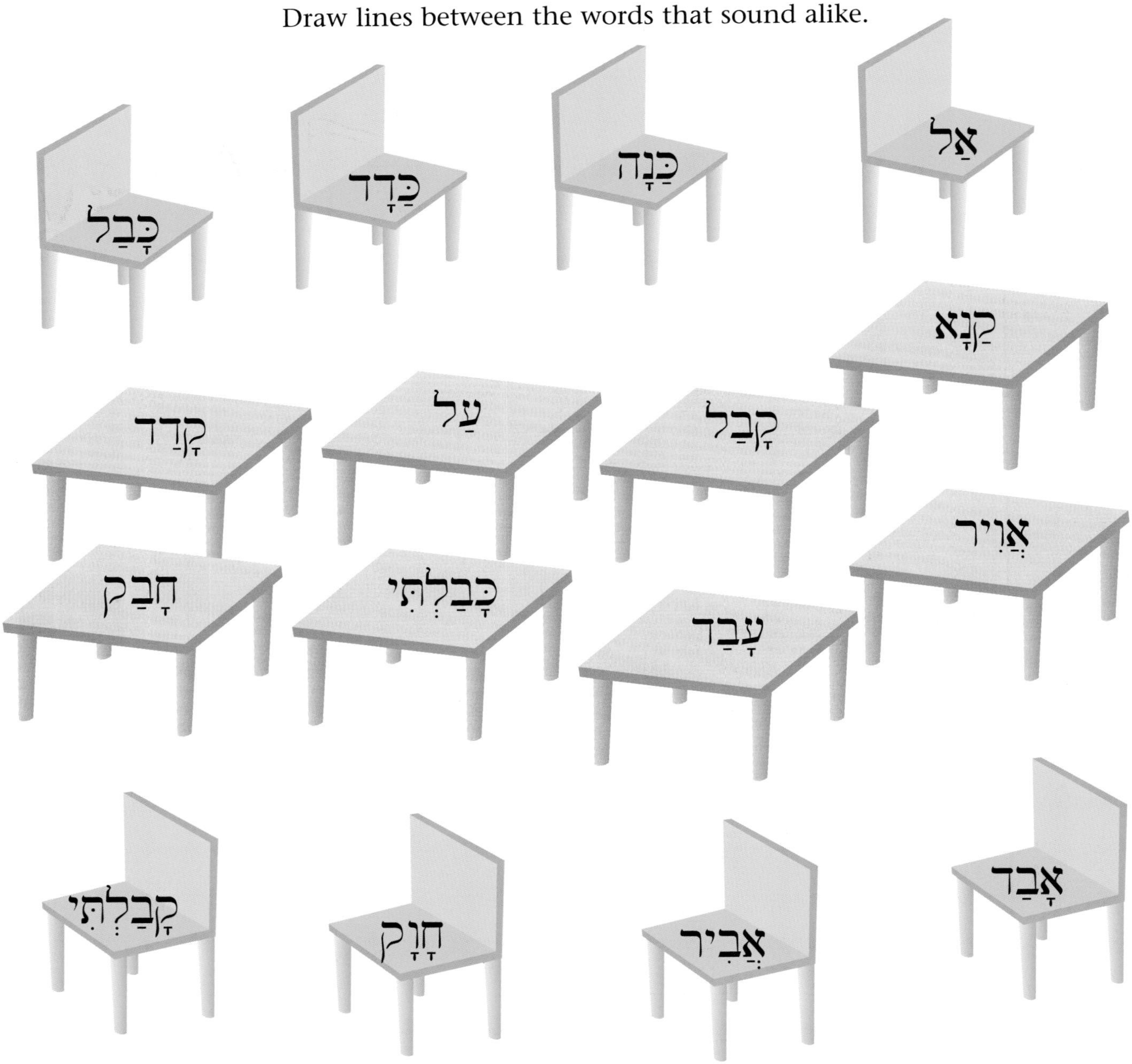

כָּבַל

כָּדַד

כָּנָה

אֵל

קָנָא

קָדַד

עַל

קָבַל

אֲוִיר

חָבַק

כָּבַלְתִּי

עָבַד

קָבַלְתִּי

חֻוק

אֲבִיר

אָבַד

76

Lesson 10
KEY WORDS:
עִבְרִית   כִּתָּה

New Vocabulary

in the classroom = בַּכִּתָּה

on = עַל

Write עַל or תַּחַת to show where the mouse is.

_____ .4   _____ .3   _____ .2   _____ .1

Write בַּבַיִת or בַּכִּתָּה under each object.

_____ .4   _____ .3   _____ .2   _____ .1

Lesson 10
KEY WORDS:
עִבְרִית כִּתָּה

New Vocabulary

next to = עַל-יַד

1. מִי בַּכִּתָּה? _____

2. מָה בַּמַיִם? _____

3. מָה בַּבַּיִת? _____

4. מָה בַּהַגָּדָה? _____

5. מִי עַל-יַד הַבַּיִת? _____

6. מָה בַּיָד? _____

7. מָה עַל-יַד הַחַלָּה? _____

Match these answers to the questions above.

דָג בַּמַיִם.

גִיר בַּיָד.

יַיִן בַּבַּיִת.

עִבְרִית בַּהַגָּדָה.

הַמִשְׁפָּחָה עַל-יַד הַבַּיִת.

יַיִן עַל-יַד הַחַלָּה.

אַבְרָהָם בַּכִּתָּה.

Lesson 10

KEY WORDS: עִבְרִית   כִּתָּה

Look at page 78 and write the line number that matches each picture.

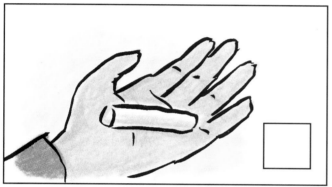

Lesson 10

KEY WORDS:

עִבְרִית כִּתָּה

PREPARE for PRAYER

Read the words in each "word family tree."

מַעֲרָב	כָּתַב	עָמַד
מַעֲרִיב	כָּתוּב	עָמְדָה
הַמַּעֲרִיב	הַכָּתוּב	עָמְדוּ
עַרְבִית	כַּכָּתוּב	עֲמִידָה
עַרְבִים	כָּתַבְתִּי	עָמַדְנוּ
בָּעֲרָבִים	כָּתַבְתְּ	מַעֲמָד

Evening   **Writing**   **Standing**

__ __ __   __ __ __   __ __ __

Fill in the roots of each tree with its matching three-letter root.

ע.מ.ד   ע.ר.ב   כ.ת.ב

Cool Hebrew Words

the standing prayer עֲמִידָה

The עֲמִידָה is one of our most important prayers.
This prayer is said while standing.

REVIEW PAGE

WORD SEARCH — Find the hidden words and write them on the lines below. Words are written right to left or top to bottom.

א	מ	א	ה	ה	ח	פּ	שׁ	מ	ר	ד
ג	ה	ב	ג	ד	ג	ב	צ	ע	ם	
י	ח	א	ד	י	ם	ת	ה	ל	ח	
ר	כ	ב	ה	י	נ	א	ב	ח	ג	
ן	פּ	כ	ת	אָ	שׁ	ת	ח	ת	ב	
שׁ	וּ	ד	ק	וּ	ג	ה	ת	כ	ב	
פּ	ר	ק	ה	וּ	צ	מ	מ	ק	י	
ת	י	ר	ב	ע	וּ	ן	י	ת		
ת	ם	י	מ	ח	ה	ל	ד	ב	ה	

1. Sabbath _____
2. fish _____
3. mother _____
4. father _____
5. read on Passover _____
6. eat on Passover _____
7. hand _____
8. I _____
9. blessing on wine _____
10. wine _____
11. Purim _____
12. challah _____
13. commandment _____

14. Hebrew _____
15. class _____
16. who _____
17. in the house _____
18. what _____
19. water _____
20. chalk _____
21. you (m.) _____
22. under _____
23. you (f.) _____
24. family _____
25. on _____
26. separation _____

EVALUATION
Lessons 1-5

	Lesson 5	Lesson 4	Lesson 3	Lesson 2	Lesson 1
.1	אֱ	צִ	אֹ	דְ	בֵּ
.2	בִי	מָא	שָׁא	תַּג	שַׁתָ
.3	נָמָה	הַשׁ	מָג	גַּדְ	בָּשֶׁ
.4	אֱגִידָה	מַגָה	אַד	דְשׁ	בַּת
.5	הָיָה	הַצָּד	מַבָּא	בַּג	שָׁת
.6	נָהַג	אֹצֵת	אָמָת	תַּשָׁד	בֵּשׁ
.7	צִיָה	שָׁהָה	דַמְשׁ	גַּדְשׁ	שָׁתַת
.8	יָמִישׁ	תָּצֵג	גָאֵת	דַבָּת	בֵּשַׁת
.9	דִינָת	שָׁאָה	אַבְּד	שָׁגַּד	שָׁתֵשׁ
.10	נִיצָה	גֵהָשׁ	תָּמְשׁ	תָּבַג	בֵּבָּת

Score _____

Date _____

EVALUATION
Lessons 6-10

	Lesson 10	Lesson 9	Lesson 8	Lesson 7	Lesson 6
1.	כָּלוּא	חַוָּה	בָּחוּשׁ	פּוּ	קוּ
2.	עָגוּם	לָוּוּ	תָּמָר	תָּרַם	הַגָּן
3.	כַּפָּרָה	בְּבַת	צְלוֹם	נַגָּר	אָנוּ
4.	עֵרִית	פָּנָיו	מָחָר	גַּפַּיִם	יָמָה
5.	עֲבָדָה	מִדְיָן	פָּגוּר	שָׁנוּי	בַּקָּשָׁה
6.	נָווֹן	חָלַצְנוּ	לָקוּם	צָמוּק	אַיִן
7.	יַשְׁכִּיב	הִקְדִּים	פָּנִים	אֲדָמָה	צִיּוּד
8.	עֲקִיצָה	פּוּרְקָן	לָחוּת	פָּקִיד	נָגוּן
9.	מַעֲבָדָה	אֲוִירָה	תִּקּוּן	רָדוּם	דָּקִיק
10.	חִכִּינוּ	נִבְחַרְתִּי	הֵדָחַת	בָּהִיר	דָּגָן

Score	

Date	

כ				**א**
כִּתָּה	(10) _____		(3) _____	אַבָּא
מ			(3) _____	אִמָּא
מַה?	(6) _____		(5) _____	אֲנִי
מִי?	(5) _____		(9) _____	אַתְּ
מַיִם	(7) _____		(8) _____	אַתָּה
מַצָּה	(4) _____			**ב**
מִצְוָה	(9) _____		(5) _____	בְּ ___
מִשְׁפָּחָה	(9) _____		(5) _____	בַּיִת
ע			(9) _____	בַּר-מִצְוָה
עִבְרִית	(10) _____		(9) _____	בַּת-מִצְוָה
עַל	(10) _____			**ג**
עַל-יַד	(10) _____		(7) _____	גִּיר
פ				**ד**
פּוּרִים	(7) _____		(2) _____	דָּג
ק				**ה**
קָדוֹשׁ	(6) _____		(4) _____	הַ ___
ר			(9) _____	הַבְדָּלָה
רַבִּי	(7) _____		(4) _____	הַגָּדָה
שׁ				**ח**
שַׁבָּת	(1) _____		(8) _____	חַלָּה
ת			(8) _____	חָתוּל
תַּחַת	(8) _____			**י**
			(5) _____	יָד
			(6) _____	יַיִן